TIMBERFRAME PLAN BOOK

TIMBERFRAME PLAN BOOK

MICHAEL MORRIS AND DICK PIROZZOLO

Photo © Rich Frutchey

GIBBS·SMITH
P
PUBLISHER

Salt Lake City

Photo © Rich Frutchey

Acknowledgment

The authors wish to thank Madeline Searle, whose knowledge, guidance, and support contributed immeasurably to this project.

First Edition

05 04 03 02 01 00   5 4 3 2 1

Published by

Gibbs Smith, Publisher

P.O. Box 667

Layton, Utah 84041

Orders: (1-800) 748-5439

Web site: **www.gibbs-smith.com**

Edited by Suzanne Taylor
Designed and produced by FORTHGEAR, Inc.
Printed and bound in China

Library of Congress Cataloging-in-Publication Data

Morris, Michael, 1947–
Timberframe plan book / Michael Morris and
Dick Pirozzolo.—1st ed.
p. cm.
ISBN 0-87905-976-1
1. Architecture, Domestic—United States—Designs and plans.
2. Wooden-frame houses—Design and construction.
I. Pirozzolo, Dick, 1944– II. Title.

NA7205 .M6795 2000

728'.37'0222—dc21

00-029144

CONTENTS

Anyone who steps inside a timberframe, or post-and-beam, home for the first time invariably comes away impressed—even a bit awed—by what is encountered. The complete structural skeleton of the home is on view, but it's not just any structure, and what a view it offers! It is like entering a strange yet beautifully natural forest where you find yourself surrounded by sturdy wood trunks, graceful limbs, and branches that soar high overhead. Put out your hand and you can feel the solidity of the posts, the rough organic surface of the wood, the harmony of the materials, the visible strength of the framework, and the skill evident in its assembly. Combined, these elements produce a dwelling as handsome as it is strong, as humble as it is proud.

There are timberframe homes that are still crafted in the timeless way by woodworking traditionalists using hand tools and methods that have changed little over the centuries. Others come from modern production shops where computer-controlled saws and milling machines turn out the sturdy, treelike posts and beams. Many "antique" timber homes are former barns or churches that have been painstakingly restored to new life by craftsmen dedicated to the art and science of preserving this unique architectural heritage.

The roots of timberframing are ancient, in part because it is an essential, elemental way to build: the first man to set a post that supported a cross-member in a lean-to was building the timberframe way, even if he wasn't using heavy timbers. As shelters grew in size, so did the posts and beams needed to support them, and a system for assembling ever-more-complex structures developed. In the process, the various components acquired names according to their place in this system—king post, hammer beam, purlin, sill, and so forth—that are still used today. Without the benefit of industrial hardware, early framers also created and refined the elegant wood-to-wood joinery techniques that remain the hallmark of timber post-and-beam construction.

GELCH HOUSE

Producer: Yankee Barn Homes

Designer: Bruce Parsons

The owners of this home wished to match the spirit of their wooded lot with the tenor of their home. Thus, an expansive deck was the first order of business in creating an easygoing bond between indoors-outdoors, making it ideal for entertaining large numbers of guests. Building the first level well above the grade level creates a deck that has a more dramatic vantage point and allows for full-sized windows on the ground level. When considering this design, devote some landscaping budget to make the area under the deck pleasant, as this will prevent it from becoming a catchall for bicycles and garden tools.

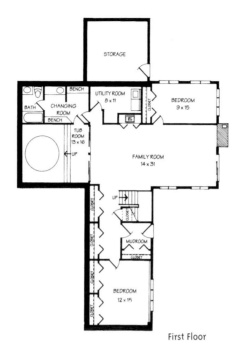

First Floor

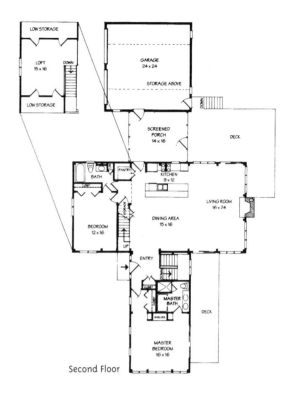

Second Floor

Photo © Suki Coughlin

Although some form of timberframing was probably employed at the dawn of civilization, it's hard to know just when this construction method really began. But we do have well-preserved examples of timber-frame structures in places as widely separated as Europe and Japan, dating as far back as the ninth century. When early settlers arrived in the New World from England, the Netherlands, Scandinavia, and Germany, they brought their post-and-beam building tools and skills with them. It wasn't long before the abundant forests of America were

When it comes to the interior, this home bespeaks "party time." The floor plan integrates the dining area and its farmer's dining table with a combination kitchen counter/snack bar. This design allows the cook and guests to mingle during food-preparation time and enables the cook to pass a few cooking chores on to guests while they gather comfortably around the bar. The magnificent floor-to-ceiling fieldstone fireplace emphasizes the open and expansive floor plan and leads the eye upward to appreciate the space.

BURGOYNE HOUSE

Producer: Yankee Barn Homes

Designer: Arne Rebne

After living and working in Saudi Arabia's oil industry for two decades, the Burgoynes decided to design and build a dream home that would give them a sense of American permanence. What could be more American than a home whose basic design is inspired by the barns that dot the countryside? Since they also wanted lots of light, they used high ceilings to create an open spacious feeling. They also decided on three stories, which gave them plenty of private spaces and ample storage and closets for their two-continent lifestyle.

Dramatic interior lighting accentuates architectural details and gives the home an overall feeling of warmth.

Photo © Suki Coughlin

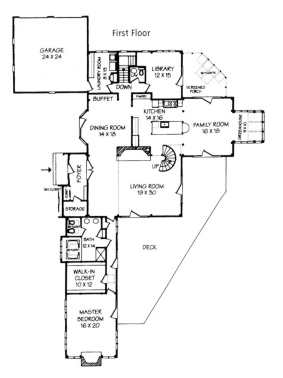

First Floor

supplying them with the timbers they needed to build this continent's first wood-framed homes.

Today's timberframe and post-and-beam homes continue to build on this heritage. Although any structure designed with posts and beams can lay claim to this title, true timberframes adhere to the traditional age-old methods of handcrafting and joinery in their architecture. Like branches of the same tree, both styles prominently display their solid, often massive, wood components. While post-and-beam construction has

The curved open staircase contrasts nicely with the massive vertical and horizontal structure of the room. The floor-to-ceiling stone fireplace leads the eye upward to emphasize both the great height and the volume of the living room.

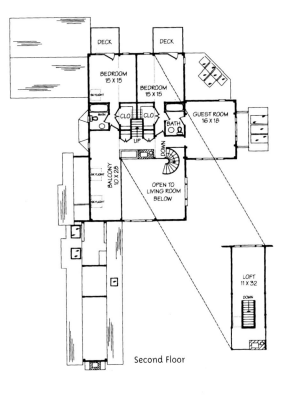

Second Floor

Photo © Suki Coughlin

always been with us to some extent, the timberframe revival in America began around the 1960s and has continued to grow among builders and buyers seeking an alternative to conventional home construction.

There are adherents to the timberframe way who won't discuss "ordinary" post-and-beam construction in the same breath. In truth, all modern timberframe homes employ technology that places them far beyond their early forebears. Overall-clad framers may still enjoy wielding heavy

This couple put the kitchen between the family room and a formal dining room. They also added a solarium at the end of the family room to bring the beauty of their wooded lot indoors.

A two-sided fireplace is a welcome addition to any home as it defines two gathering spots of equal stature and comfort. In this case, the fireplace sheds a warm glow in both the great room and the living room, doubling its benefit at a fraction of the cost of two fireplaces. In addition, the strategic location of the fireplace adds warmth and comfort to the second level.

Photo © Suki Coughlin

Producer: Yankee Barn Homes

This home's vernacular saltbox shape takes the space normally given to the kitchen and incorporates a sun-splashed space for cheerful gatherings among friends and family. The floor plan incorporates every possible type of room needed to accommodate today's growing family, including a media room, computer room, mudroom, children's retreat, and three generously proportioned bedrooms.

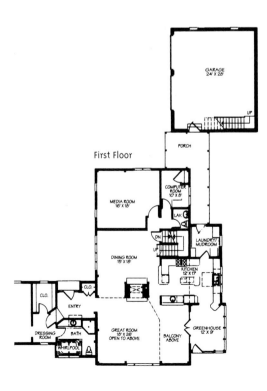

First Floor

mallets while they pound hardwood pegs into the joints, just like in the old days, but more often than not the framework itself is designed on a computer-aided program and cut by computer-controlled machinery. Construction codes also demand such innovations as energy-efficient windows, structural insulated panels, and metal anchors for security against wind and earthquakes.

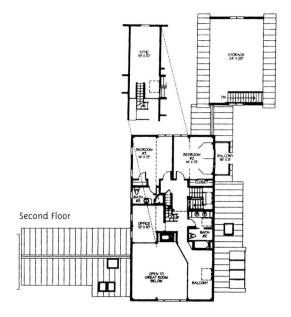

Second Floor

This book offers examples of both timber-frame and post-and-beam construction. You'll also find information that can help you make the buying and building decisions you'll need to create your own home. The timberframe way is not one path but many. Hopefully, our efforts will lead you in a direction that is right for you.

Michael Morris & Dick Pirozzolo

A corner fireplace punctuates this master bedroom, which was built into an ell on the first floor to create a home that is ideal for one-floor living but has plenty of space for weekend guests.

Left: Like many post-and-beam designs, this home integrates the semi-private loft area into the great room to create a unified whole. Note how the single window wall sheds light on both the lower and upper stories, further integrating the interior volume.

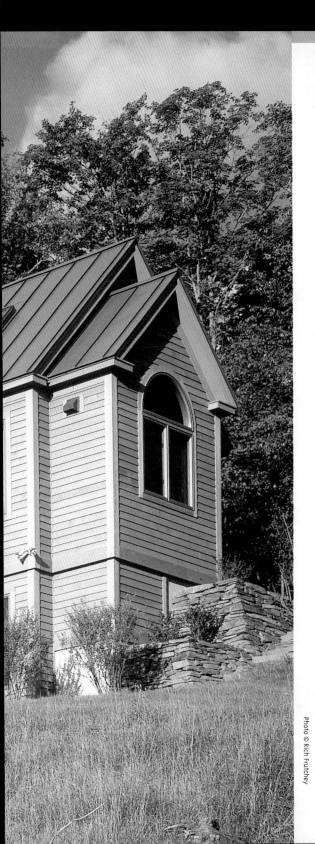

Photo © Rich Frutchey

The woodwork that makes up a timberframe home is designed as much for its handsome, graceful symmetry as for its strength and longevity. Its rugged posts and beams are invariably left fully exposed, giving interiors an architectural grandeur that surprises and delights, while providing the structure upon which the rest of the home is built. By contrast, conventional "stick-built" homes—made with studs, joists, and rafters fashioned from dressed, or dimensional, lumber—have a wood framework that is meant to be hidden beneath drywall, paneling, and other finished materials.

According to standard lumber classifications, a timber is a length of wood with a dimensional cross-section greater than five inches on each side. Of course, the posts and beams that make up a timber-frame can be, and usually are, considerably larger. Mill construction—a specific fire-code designation—calls for even larger structural wood-frame members starting at a minimum of eight inches on a side. (Because heavy, solid-wood beams char slowly rather than burn up, they are fire-resistant to some extent and provide a dependable means of fire rating for insurance purposes.) However, post-and-beam is often used as a general descriptive term without specific size or strength limits. A post is simply a vertical wood member, and beams are horizontal components.

When it comes to actual construction, the terms timberframing and post-and-beam framing are virtually synonymous, but there is a subtle difference between the two. Post-and-beam structures are more expedient in their design and assembly. Commonly available materials such as laminated, or "engineered," lumber may be used, and the components are typically fastened with stainless-steel carriage bolts, brackets, and other modern fasteners. Timberframing, on the other hand, evokes this centuries-old building craft and refers as much to its art as its construction. The timbers are often cut and dressed by hand, jointed and interlocked in the traditional way, and fastened throughout with wood pegs called trunnels, or "tree nails." On occasion, special hardware may be required by local building codes or to ensure strength in a particular joint, but the framers work hard to de-emphasize its presence. "We

HILLSIDE HAVEN

Producer: Davis Frame Company

Builder: G.H. Ware, Inc.

A custom home should reflect the homeowner's taste and lifestyle within a functional floor plan and attractive exterior. This home was designed for a couple who wanted to retire in Arizona but keep their roots in Vermont. At first, they tried a modest condo, but soon realized they needed more space to accommodate their children and grandchildren as well as their many friends still in the area. The 4,200-square-foot home has plenty of daylight and an exterior style that is reminiscent of the many farmhouses that dot the Green Mountain State.

Photo © Rich Frutchey

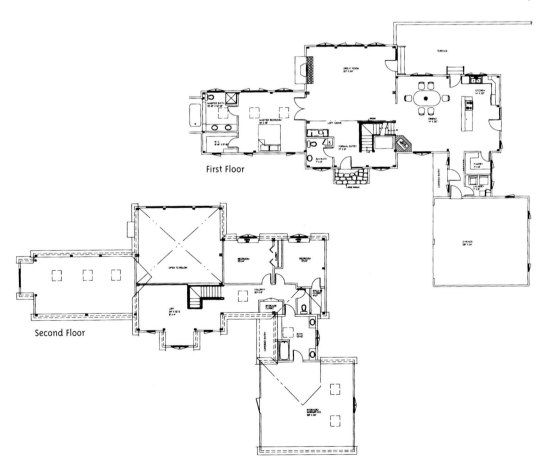

First Floor

Second Floor

The floor plan includes a 24 x 32-foot great room with plenty of room for entertaining. Despite its size, there are no supporting posts that normally would have to go in a room such as this. Davis achieved this by using an extra-large support beam, which eliminated the need for columns. The room has a large fireplace—fashioned from fieldstones from the couple's land—with a generous hearth.

DUFFY-STERLING HOUSE

Producer: Habitat Post & Beam

Designer: Jeffery C. Linfert

This basic home appears more modest than its nearly 3,000 square feet. In addition, these owners opted for a large garage with a second-story loft that serves as an office. The space was designed with a knee wall for extra headroom, and there is a connecting area with a staircase that leads from the first floor to the loft. This makes it a workspace that allows business visitors to enter without having to pass through the living quarters or the garage.

First Floor

Second Floor

Photo © Habitat Post & Beam

use mostly mortise-and-tenon joints in our frames," explains Richard Neroni of Timberpeg Homes. "When we have to use metal hardware, it's usually for some complex reason, and then we use things like hidden bolt-connectors that are buried deep in the wood so they're never seen."

Timberframes use less wood than comparably sized, conventional stick-frame homes, but they are elegant in their simplicity and immensely strong for their fewer parts. Depending on the frame's complexity, the size of its timbers, and the owner's wishes, a timber structure can include anywhere from several

The delicate balusters of the open staircase contrast nicely with the massive Douglas fir timbers. The ceiling is completed in 2 x 6" tongue-and-groove cedar.

dozen to several hundred individual pieces. The framework is designed like a web to transfer the load, or weight, of the entire structure and everything within it—the timbers, other building materials, snow and rain, interior furnishings, and the occupants—to the ground via the most efficient route. This weight is ultimately carried by the main posts, so most timberframes are "point-loaded" structures. Conventional homes, with their network of thousands of interconnected lumber pieces, are referred to as "distributed-load" structures.

Because timbers can carry enormous loads and can span greater distances than conventional building lumber, they allow for much larger unsupported interior spaces. It's not unusual to see timberframes with vast open areas stretching from one exterior wall to another and reaching upward two or three stories to a vaulted roof. In fact, cathedral ceilings are a hallmark of timberframes simply because they are

Despite the volume of this two-story interior space, the design has the snugness of a tightly built New England colonial home. This overall effect is attributed to the selection of materials such as fieldstone for the fireplace, finely milled railings, and traditional décor. The loft floor doubles as a low ceiling over the dining area, defining the space and giving it an intimate feeling.

CLASSIC YORK

Producer: Classic Post & Beam

This is a true classic colonial with two floors plus extra living space on the third level. Its style is in the New England center-entrance colonial tradition, which calls for an ample foyer with a living room to the left and dining room to the right. The kitchen runs along the rear. This style has endured since the eighteenth century and remains popular because it works so well for any occasion—from casual daily living to a formal dinner party for twelve. The home demonstrates a useful design idea when it comes to enhancing curb appeal—move the overhead garage doors to the side and add a woodbin on the front. The home is a model for the manufacturer and is located just north of Kittery, Maine, on Historic Route 1. It is open to visitors seven days a week.

Photo © Classic Post & Beam

First Floor

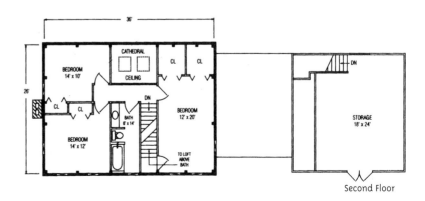

Second Floor

A cozy fire and exposed ceiling beams make this home a snug winter retreat.

CLASSIC COLONIAL

Producer: Davis Frame Company

Designer: James Gray

With over a hundred windows, this home could be mistaken for a quaint bed and breakfast with lots of comfortable rooms. The sidelights and gracefully arched window above the front entrance make the foyer more impressive. It opens to a grand space with a twenty-seven-foot-high ceiling passing over two lofts.

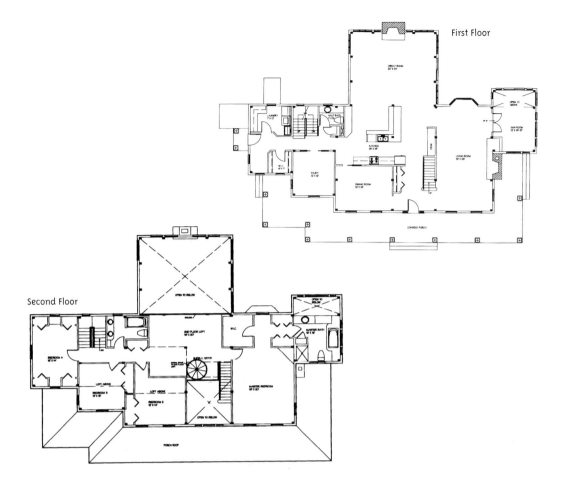

First Floor

Second Floor

Photo © Rich Frutchey

so easy to create. And with the framework carrying virtually the entire building load, interior load-bearing walls are often not required. Only non-load-bearing partition walls are needed to enclose private spaces like bedrooms and baths, or for plumbing, electrical wiring, heating, and air-conditioning-duct access.

ANATOMY

You don't have to understand the function or be able to identify every part of a timberframe to appreciate its beauty. However, owners take great pride in their timber homes, which

A formal grand staircase with white balusters and contrasting natural-wood accents enhances the classic colonial look of this home. Note the third-floor loft, which is accessible by a spiral staircase.

Photo © Rich Frutchey

are often custom-designed with unique arrangements of posts, beams, and other framing options. It's not unusual for frame makers to ask the buyers how they envision their interior framework— Gothic, churchlike, reserved, dramatic, or even sleek and modern. Some owners prefer more complex interiors, while others seek understatement and quiet strength. "We try to determine how much wood a buyer wants to see and then design it for them," says Debbie Davis of the Davis Frame Company.

Knowing one timber from another and having at least some understanding of the role each post and beam plays in the entire system are part of the enjoyment of owning and living in these unique structures. In fact, there are fewer than a dozen principal parts in timberframes, with variations of each used in specific circumstances. Armed with this information, you'll be able to see

In addition to the great room, the architects included a more intimate seating area with a flat ceiling and traditional fireplace. The colonial furnishings and décor, along with curtains, further define this space as a retreat for reading or quiet conversation.

CIOPPA HOUSE

Producer: Pacific Post & Beam

Designer: Bennett Christopherson

Builder: Stuart Wentworth

When this homeowner had an opportunity to build a home of her own, she replicated the aura of the Pasadena bungalow where she lived as a child. The modest home is less than 1,700 square feet with the master bedroom suite on the main floor and a guest room and study on the 600 square-foot second level. The home's understated good looks can be attributed to a simple vernacular style implemented with superb craftsmanship and recycled materials.

Photo © Joseph Kasparowitz

First Floor

these structures the way architects and builders do—as individual parts that make up a greater whole.

The legs of every timberframe are its posts, and in most cases they are designed simply to carry the weight of the structure. Early builders fashioned their posts from whole trees, occasionally turning them upside down and utilizing the natural flare at the base of the trunk as a wide resting shelf for the beams they supported. Posts made this way are called joweled, or gunstock, posts. Often a king post is used to tie several beams together and never touches a floor or rests on any other base. It extends downward

The lofty roofline and open truss above the kitchen cabinets enhance the feeling of openness in an otherwise tight yet efficient working area. The quality and the polished countertop give the kitchen a no-nonsense look that culinary enthusiasts crave.

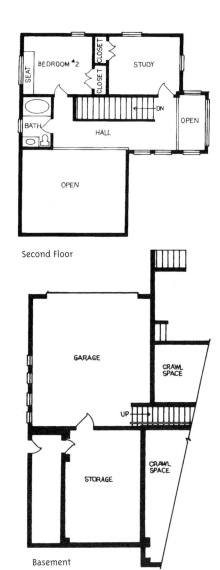

Second Floor

Basement

from the roof ridge and forms an intersection with horizontal beams. A variation on this is the queen post, which is generally used in pairs to support wide spans.

Beams are all horizontal timbers, but they are somewhat more specialized than posts and have an equally varied nomenclature. A timber sill is a beam often used as the base of a structure, forming a perimeter upon which the main posts stand. Girts, from which we get the word "girder," are the main beams that span the entire length or width of a frame. Summer beams stretch between girts and reduce larger spans so shorter joists can be used to support the floors. Horizontal purlins are used to reinforce

The colors and textures of these materials reflect the Arts & Crafts era that inspired this home. This fireplace was done in clinker bricks, which were once discarded because their variegated shapes were considered imperfections. The beams were crafted of recycled timbers. The interplay of these rough textures is in sharp contrast to the smooth bird's-eye-maple floors and Craftsman-style furnishings.

CHANDLER HOUSE

Producer: Lindal Cedar Homes

This roofline boasts a clerestory, another small roof extending above the primary roof that includes several small windows. This architectural detail serves several purposes beyond its decorative value. The high windows bring light into the upper part of the structure, which is particularly important in large-volume interiors. Opening the windows (which can be automated if they are out of reach) will create a natural "chimney effect" that draws stale air from throughout the house, exhausting it along with any heat buildup under the roof peak. It is ideal in an open setting.

First Floor

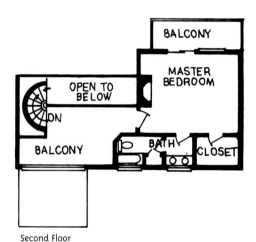

Second Floor

exterior posts, to tie roof sections together, or to replace rafters when the distance between the ridge and walls is too great.

A principal element in every timberframe is the bent, which is an assembly of posts and beams that make up a cross-section of a frame. A bent looks like a one-dimensional child's drawing of a house. Another way to look at bents is to envision them as slices of bread in a loaf, each one extending completely through the structure from one side of the frame to the other, often reaching from the foundation to the ridge. Each end-wall is a bent, and between each pair of bents is a bay. Timber bents are typically built flat on the slab or deck, then raised in place one by one. In earlier times, a crew of willing neighbors would bend their backs to this task (as accurately depicted in the movie *Witness*, starring Harrison Ford), although today a crane or site-rigged "gin pole" is more often used, especially when the bents are too heavy to lift by manpower alone. Once upright, the bents are temporarily braced until the girts, joists, and other beams can be installed to lock the frame into a unified whole.

Another often-used timber assembly is the truss, which has a purely functional purpose but is also created to serve as an interior focal point of many timberframe homes. Constructed

As an alternative to contrasting beams and posts, this home's monochromatic interior focuses on the benefits of post and beam—space and volume—rather than the structural elements.

in various ways, trusses employ geometry to transfer the weight of a roof or other upper-story sections, such as balconies and lofts, to the walls without any support from below. A king-post truss, for example, is made up of a horizontal girt, or collar tie, with an integral center post that supports the ridge. Angle braces are often added between the girt and principal rafters, or from post to ridge, for stability. Scissor trusses form an elongated X across wide spans and are very efficient at carrying loads without support posts. Perhaps the most elegant form of a timber truss is the hammer-beam truss, which relies on a complex, stacked arrangement of short beams and braces to span large areas without any beams extending through the open area.

The hallmark of timberframing can be seen in its joinery. Interlocking wood-to-wood joints, most of them developed in the Middle Ages, are used not only to connect the heavy timbers but also to lend strength and transfer the load efficiently to the other posts and beams. Many

Sun spaces are inviting and are a great way to bring in lots of natural light and awe-inspiring views. They can also help warm the home by heating tile and other surfaces—including even bathroom fixtures.

The practice of breaking up large glass areas with grilles to create divided lights is inspired by New England colonial architecture that dates back to a time when panes were made by glassblowers in modest dimensions. The grille pattern is in perfect harmony with the larger pattern established in the structural posts and beams.

CARTER HOUSE

Producer: Yankee Barn Homes

Designer: Jim Wheeler

This grand getaway on Block Island, off the coast of Rhode Island, incorporates two distinct looks—a beach house and a traditional farmhouse. Expansive windows throughout take full advantage of 360-degree views of this New England summer playground.

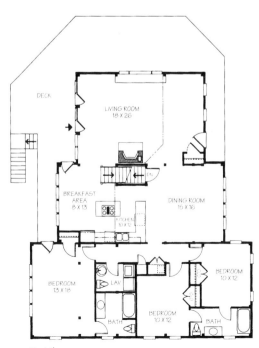

First Floor

frame assemblies today are precut with precision machinery, but some framers still cut these joints by hand, using mallets and chisels along with hand-operated power tools. According to Frank Baker of Riverbend Timber Framing, "We use more automated machinery now, but from the beginning we have always relied mainly on hand-cutting and -finishing for our frames."

The most common timber woodworking joints are the same as those found in fine furniture, and include mortise-and-tenon, dovetail, half-lap, and scarf joints. In some cases, holes are

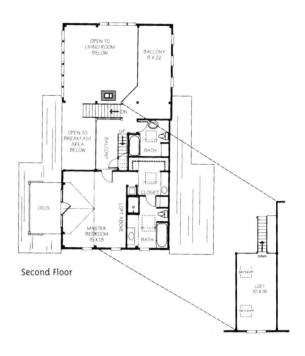

Second Floor

bored through the joints, and hardwood pegs—or trunnels—are pounded in to reinforce and permanently secure them. One can only stare in amazement at massive constructions like the cathedrals and public buildings built this way several hundred years ago that are still in service and as sturdy as ever.

Despite its heritage and time-honored building traditions, timberframing continues to evolve—in part because it is so specialized, but also because building one of these homes can be expensive. To keep costs down, some framers now offer "optimized," or "hybrid," timber-frame structures that use less-costly materials for basic structural sections, placing timbers only where they are necessary and most visible.

A generous dormer breaks up the plane of the roofline on the exterior and adds character to the master bedroom.

The owners were also able to build a sundeck—a fine spot for capturing ocean views.

MARLING HOUSE

Producer: Hearthstone, Inc.

Designer: Richard Merlie

The frame of this 7,000-square-foot home in Madison, Wisconsin, was crafted using mortise-and-tenon joinery secured with more than 1,800 wood pegs and not a single metal fastener. Many timberframers buy all their pegs from Scott Northcut of Walpole, New Hampshire, who makes more than 400,000 of them annually out of kiln-dried white oak turned on antique lathes and cut to the exact lengths ordered by the timber-framer. To Northcut's credit, he has contributed his pegs to numerous charitable home-building projects organized by the Timberframers Guild.

Photo © Don Kerkhof

If designed carefully, these non-timber areas will not detract from the beauty of the timberframe and will bring these homes within reach of more buyers. As long as the builders understand that it is the wood and the joinery that buyers want to see, there will always be timberframes cut and raised the "old-fashioned" way.

JOINERY

The skill and handiwork that goes into traditional timberframe joinery is a marvel to behold. At once simple and complex, these wood-to-wood joints evolved out of pure necessity—the early framers didn't have ready access to metal hardware, so they invented their own methods of connecting the heavy posts and beams. Some of these joinery techniques were developed by one culture and eventu-ally passed along or absorbed by craftsmen in other lands. Even today, frame styles and their joinery are identified by the nationalities that created them.

With so many timbers coming together in one spot, craftsmanship is what really gives this joinery its aesthetic appeal. In this case, girts, which are the beams that link the bents, or sections, are inserted into a housing on the vertical post. Girts rest on a shoulder on the post and are secured with a mortise-and-tenon joint.

First Floor

Second Floor

Perhaps the real marvel is that time has shown these methods to be every bit as good as, if not far superior to, most modern-construction fastening systems. A proper timber joint not only ties the wood together, it also transfers the load carried by one post or beam along to the next, creating frames that amount to incredibly strong and durable unified assemblies. Although there are only a few principal types of joints—mainly the dovetail, mortise-and-tenon, and scarf—there are dozens of variations on each type. Often, these variations serve a special purpose or are found only in particular

When juxtaposing stone and wood, keep these elements in more-or-less-equal scale to balance the look. The large stones of this fireplace are in keeping with the heft of the beams.

Furniture plays an active role in the open floor plan of a timberframe home by defining space.

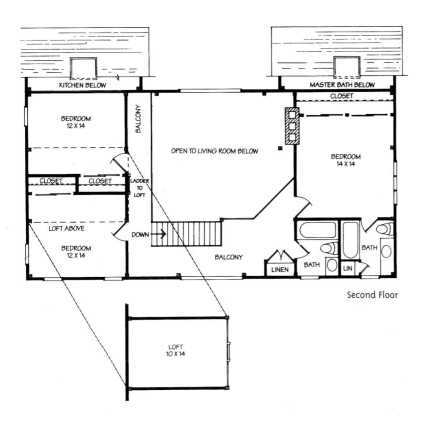

KITCHEN BELOW

MASTER BATH BELOW

CLOSET

BEDROOM
12 X 14

BALCONY

OPEN TO LIVING ROOM BELOW

BEDROOM
14 X 14

CLOSET   CLOSET

LADDER
TO
LOFT

LOFT ABOVE

DOWN →

BATH

BEDROOM
12 X 14

BALCONY

LINEN

BATH

LIN

BATH

Second Floor

LOFT
10 X 14

LENNOX HOUSE

Producer: Yankee Barn Homes

Designer: Bruce Parsons

This understated home offers plenty of room in a traditional design for a large family. The double door, with a half-round window above, reduces the massiveness of the façade. With this much wood, it is important to minimize maintenance chores by using a good-quality stain rather than paint, which can flake and peel and has to be scraped before a new coat can be applied. Keep foundation plantings to a minimum and as far away from the home as practical. Gutters and leaders are essential to prevent mud from splashing against the house.

places in a frame. The following is just a sampling of the major terms used in this craft.

BEETLE—A large, heavy wooden mallet used to hammer joints tight and "coax" timbers into position; also called a commander, this tool has a long, sledge-like handle, and its mallet head is often fashioned from a natural log and banded with metal rings to prevent it from splitting.

BIRDSMOUTH—A notch cut near the bottom end of a rafter that allows it to sit flush on the wall's top plate. It also refers specifically to a cut made in one timber that makes it fit tightly over another.

Photo © Yankee Barn Homes

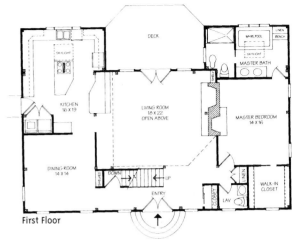

First Floor

BOX—The practice of shaving or planing a tenon, or post end, to fit into a mortised socket; also refers to a dovetail-like joint with squared pins.

DOVETAIL—A joint with an interlocking pin, or tenon, that fits into a matching socket; also used in fine furniture joinery.

DRAW BORE—The practice of drilling holes slightly out of line through a mortise-and-tenon joint so that when the hardwood pegs are pounded home, they draw the joint together.

HAUNCH—A term that generally means to thicken or add support. In timber joinery it refers to (1) the wide resting shelf of a gunstock, or joweled, post, and (2) an extension or shoulder at the end of a tenoned beam that adds support to the joint by resting in a recess cut in the face of a mortised post.

Though the exterior of this home has the look and feel of Longfellow's Wayside Inn on The Old Boston Post Road, its interior draws elements from more temperate zones.

Left: The wide-slat wood blinds and casement windows in this room emit a tropical feel. When installing casement windows that crank out (unlike double-hung windows that open upward), consider whether there are walkways below where people are apt to hit their heads when the windows are open.

THE KOEPPEL

Producer: Classic Post & Beam

When Beth and Tom Koeppel approached Classic Post & Beam, the couple had an idea of what they wanted—a classic colonial with Victorian elements. The combination gives the home stylish high notes that include a three-sided bump-out on the façade, an oval window in the master bedroom, and ornate front-porch balusters. On the interior, the bump-out makes the dining room and master bedroom directly above it more spacious and elegant. Many manufacturers boast superb design departments and, recognizing that planning a home is an evolutionary process, offer customers numerous revisions without added cost. When it came to budgeting, Beth carefully researched building and finishing materials and kept detailed records on light fixtures, flooring, and siding. In this case, the couple chose Cape Cod Siding, which is prestained on both sides and arrives with its own prestained nails.

Photo © Rich Frutchey

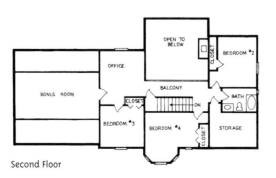

First Floor

Second Floor

LAP—One side of a timber splice or scarf joint, often referred to as a half-lap; generally used to lay one material or section atop another.

KEY—A wedge-shaped wood pin inserted into a tenon end, or joint, to lock timbers together and prevent movement.

MORTISE—A pocket bored into one timber to receive a matching tenon cut onto the end of an intersecting timber; mortise-and-tenon joints usually have squared, closely fitting faces that intersect at right angles.

The Victorian-style bump-out offers a cozy seating area in the master bedroom and a place for Tom to keep up with his passion—playing the banjo.

Photo © Rich Frutchey

POCKET—A general term that refers to any recess cut into one timber to receive another.

SCANTLING—A rough-sawn timber; also refers to a dimensional lumber stud, or any long thin piece of wood.

SCARF—A splice or lap joint, often used to extend the length of a beam made up of two or more timbers.

SEAT—To securely fit one timber into or on another; also refers to a shoulder or ledge cut into a vertical wood member that helps support an intersecting horizontal timber.

In many construction schedules, the typical budgets for light fixtures are stingy. If you have a formal dining room and lighting budgets are tight, splurge on the chandelier. It is the focal point of an important room where families gather for holidays and other events.

In addition to the Thimble Islands, numerous hull-ripping rocks lurk just at or beneath the water's surface, making it necessary for the locals to "learn the rocks" as children. The highly textural surface of the fireplace reflects a sense of that environment and the nearby community of Stony Creek.

SHIM—A thin, usually tapered, flat slice of wood inserted or pounded into joints to take up excess space, tighten the joint, and prevent movement between the wood members.

SPIKE—A general term that refers to any large metal nail or pin, or the act of fastening with nails.

TENON—A narrow projection cut onto the end of a timber that fits into a matching socket or mortise.

THROUGH-MORTISE—A pocket that extends completely through a timber; stopped-mortise refers to a shallow pocket cut to receive a stub tenon.

TONGUE-AND-GROOVE—A long shallow joint that generally runs the full length of the materials it connects and usually used on sheet materials. Half of the joint is cut to a projecting profile approximately one-third the overall width and fits into a corresponding groove, or kerf, on the intersecting piece.

TRUNNEL—Originally "tree nail," a large hardwood peg inserted into holes bored into or through intersecting

DUO DICKINSON HOUSE

Producer: Habitat Post & Beam

Designer: Phillip George

Architect: Duo Dickinson

This home boasts a remarkable location—one of Long Island Sound's Thimble Islands, where legendary pirate Captain Kidd hid from authorities. To this day, residents of that particular Thimble Island paint all their homes black and fly the Jolly Roger as homage to its renegade past. When this spectacular home was built, a giant helicopter was used to fly in hoppers full of concrete to pour the foundation. A five-foot-deep underwater tunnel was also burrowed for the sanitary system, water, and utilities to make the home habitable year-round. The home has a copper standing-ridge roof and a vast wall of glass, making it a standout among island retreats. It is but one example of the extraordinary lengths to which people will go to build and live on the Thimbles and is testament to a collaborative effort between architect, timberframe manufacturer, and numerous other craftspeople who turned this engineering marvel into a reality.

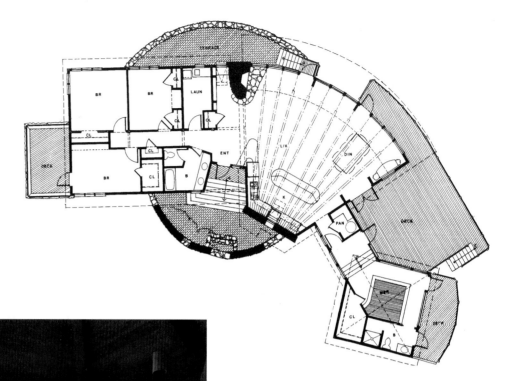

timbers and used to permanently lock the joint together; also called pegs.

TUSK TENON—A stepped projection that extends out the back side of a through-mortise, where it can be locked into place with a key; this joint is often used to pull intersecting load-bearing timbers together or to prevent them from splaying, as with floor joists.

TYING JOINT—A complex post-top joint used to support and join the top wall plate with an intersecting tie beam; often found in traditional old-world timberframes, it is identified by double and sometimes triple vertical tenons.

This twenty-five-foot-high wall contains more than thirty windows that were built in sections at a nearby site and airlifted in by a helicopter that also served as an aerial crane, holding the panels erect while workers bolted them in place.

Photo © Brad Simmons

Timberframe homes are "at home" anywhere. In a suburban neighborhood, any exterior can be selected so it blends with conventionally framed homes. It's only when one enters the front door that its beauty is revealed—an interior that is open, with a soaring cathedral ceiling and natural light among sturdy timbers.

You may also find the perfect site for your timberframe home to be far from neighbors in a wooded setting, on an island of your own, or in an abandoned orchard or open field. If your site happens to be remote it may mean blazing a road to allow materials and equipment to follow. It means using non-traditional methods—and large doses of resourcefulness—to get things done. This can save money, but it can increase costs in other ways. Builders charge more when they have to travel or tie up equipment at a remote site, or simply because they're unsure of the pitfalls they may (or may not) encounter. And there are other considerations. Power, water, and sewer systems, for example, generally cost more and have to be budgeted accordingly.

On the positive side: once completed, your dream home will be far from neighbors, traffic noise, and the hustle of life. So if your heart is set on building a home in glorious natural surroundings, don't be deterred—the rewards are too great.

BUILDING WITH A KIT

Start researching your project early to find a manufacturer who specializes in the type of frame construction you have in mind. No matter what your dream home will look like, how small or how big, there is a long list of companies that can provide any kind of timber structure you desire. And you can order it any way you want it.

A good way to cut down on time, work, and materials is to choose a kit structure for your building program. A kit with any number of precut, prefabricated parts helps simplify things, which in turn helps you stay on schedule and within budget. When every stick and nail has to be hauled to a distant or dif-

THOMPSON HOUSE

Producer: Oakbridge Timber Framing

Though it offers its owners more than 4,000 square feet of open living space, the curbside view is one of a modest home that belies its capacious interior. The couple chose Oakbridge as its manufacturer, as this is an Amish-owned company that hearkens back to community barn-raising traditions and produces about a dozen homes per year. The principal owner, John Miller, learned timberframing from his father, who learned it from his father. Though its roots are planted deep in Amish country, Oakbridge is a dealer for Fischer SIPS, or Structural Insulated Panels. These sandwiches of plywood, or oriented strand-board, and rigid insulation are what most modern timberframe homes are enclosed with to create an energy-efficient envelope that is right for the twenty-first century.

First Floor

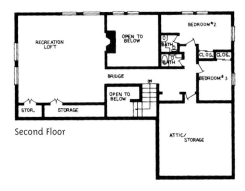

Second Floor

Photo © Brad Simmons

ficult-to-reach site, you're better off with fewer pieces that need to be cut, constructed, or accounted for once you unload. And with a building package, you won't have to run to town so often for things you need or items you forgot.

Building kits vary widely in what they include. You can choose a basic frame-only kit and complete the conventional stages of construction by yourself or with help from a local builder. If you opt for a timberframe shell, you'll also be provided with such materials such as plywood, windows, doors, and roof shingles required to protect the frame in a weather-tight—although far from finished—enclosure. Or you can buy so-called "turnkey" packages that include all of the other construction and finish components, such as kitchen cabinets, bath fixtures, and flooring—virtually everything you need to complete your home.

Carefully reviewing what each manufacturer includes and comparing prices at the outset will help you determine where difficulties and cost overruns might creep in later. And you can customize the "packages" offered by the manufacturers. Companies that supply all components will usually credit buyers for any materials that they wish to purchase through their own suppliers. If you do this, be aware that it may only seem less expensive to purchase a frame-only kit and then head for your local home center to buy

The catwalk and staircase define the intimate dining area on the first floor.

YOUNG HOUSE

Producer: Lindal Cedar Homes

Bob and Sally Young opted for a custom home by Lindal, which includes personal spaces to accommodate both work and hobbies. Bob, a freelance artist, writer, and illustrator, has a place set up for computer work that is private enough to concentrate and yet public enough to not feel isolated. He also incorporated a studio with plenty of northern light. Sally, who volunteers as a storyteller, created a loft area with children's books and characters she uses for this activity.

This home has a California-bungalow look curbside and a prow to the rear. The prow is an architectural style that is not unique to Lindal Homes, but it has become this manufacturer's signature design. Whether sited on a lake, seashore, meadow, or woods, prows provide stunning views when fitted with floor-to-peak windows. Though many of this company's homes are trophy residences today, the founder of Lindal, Sir Walter Lindal, was a pioneer in the premanufactured kit-home industry during the post-World War II building boom and helped many young couples buy their first homes. Lindal offers many energy-efficient features and makes good use of the rich, abundant western red cedar grown in the Pacific Northwest.

Photo © Lindal Cedar Homes

First Floor

Second Floor

This plan was modified from a Craftsman model. Its front offers plenty of glass to take advantage of the view of rolling hills outside San Luis Obispo, California. Lindal incorporates engineering and design services as part of its packages. The company will work with the homeowner's architect, modify an existing plan, or create an entirely new one.

Photo © Roger Wade

WILLERT HOUSE

Designer/Builder: Dan Pauroso, HP Woodworking

Architect: Danny Eagan

Architect Danny Eagan brings together a range of traditional building materials to create an exterior that visually communicates the casual easy living of this home on sixty acres in Idaho. Among the materials used are rough-hewn fir planks contrasted with old-fashioned chinking made of durable modern materials. The chimney and portions of the façade are faced in fieldstone. Split-cedar roofing shakes and copper flashing continue the subtle tones—all of which contrast nicely with red window trim. Located in the Teton Valley region with the Big Hole Mountain Range to the west, this is a perfect spot to view breathtaking sunsets. Note how the post-and-beam elements on the front porch reflect the nature of the interior structure. Eagan has created a Cotswold cottage that, despite its modest size, is indeed roomy and comfortable.

all of the other materials at "discount" prices. Unless you have the experience and dedication needed to make this strategy work, the extra effort and hidden costs that may result can make any savings on the basic frame quickly evaporate while increasing the time it takes to close in the home. On the other hand, buying a complete kit that has all of the components included in one price and delivered at one time will not only save you time, but can make the overall cost more predictable. The choice is yours, but it should be carefully considered and will depend largely on your timetable and the level of involvement you intend to have in the project.

Says Jim Nadeau, of Classic Post & Beam, "Manufactured kits can save you time and money in other ways. The frames, which on average contain 150 or so individual posts and beams, are cut and test-assembled at the factory, then disassembled for shipping. This ensures that the complex joinery will fit together properly when delivered to your building site." As many framers can attest, it can make a

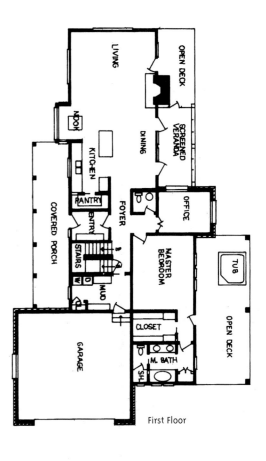

First Floor

Photo © Roger Wade

building project quick, trouble-free, and satisfying. It's not unusual for even large complicated frames to be assembled on-site in a matter of hours and enclosed within a week.

Timberframe kits are available from a variety of sources. Larger manufacturers often provide design, architectural, and engineering services, as well as optional on-site technical guidance and construction supervision.

There are also individual craft builders who cut and sell only a few frames per year and personally raise every frame with their own crews. The size of the company and the way they conduct their operation matters less than whether they enjoy a well-established reputation for quality and reliability. Ask to speak with homeowners who have built the company's kits—these references are generally reliable, and the owners are usually happy to share their building experiences.

The wood ceiling and floor-to-ceiling windows are gracefully arched in striking contrast to the right angles and massive wood structure of this home. Compare the difference in texture between the smooth grain of the ceiling and the rough-hewn structural elements and mantel. No attempt to hide the carriage-bolt fasteners is made, giving the home a substantial and secure look.

This large interior space demonstrates that design need not always be symmetrical. Notice how an oval window adds impact to the overall setting. Another good use of space is to flank the fireplace with built-in bookshelves that can be used to display literature and artifacts reflecting the owner's personality.

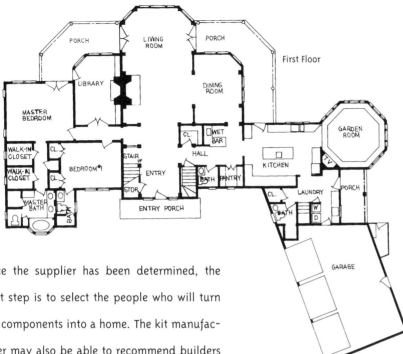

PORCH — LIVING ROOM — PORCH

First Floor

LIBRARY

DINING ROOM

MASTER BEDROOM

CL. WET BAR

GARDEN ROOM

WALK-IN CLOSET

WALK-IN CLOSET

CL.

CL.

BEDROOM #1

STAIR UP

ENTRY

HALL

KITCHEN

TV

MASTER BATH

BATH

STOR.

BATH PANTRY

CL.

LAUNDRY

PORCH

ENTRY PORCH

BATH

W D

GARAGE

Once the supplier has been determined, the next step is to select the people who will turn the components into a home. The kit manufacturer may also be able to recommend builders in your area who have already worked with their system and can proceed efficiently. When asking for such recommendations, make sure the relationship between the builder and the manufacturer is established at the outset. In some cases it will only be a recommendation, and any mistakes made by the builder will be exclusively the builder's responsibility. In other cases, the manufacturer may take on the responsibility for erecting the frame. Be sure that the company providing the kit will guarantee its product if problems arise and is willing to work with you and the builder to solve them.

Keep in mind that with any building project there will be frustrations—materials won't arrive on schedule, a window is broken, storms blow in at the worst possible times, an early

SUESSER HOUSE

Producer: Vermont Timberframes

This home's Victorian-inspired exterior gives no hint of the modern, expansive, and open interior that includes a vaulted, two-story, octagon-shaped room. Today's home designer has access to a wealth of Victorian-style elements, including windows by Andersen, finishing touches by Restoration Hardware, and kitchen cabinet makers who will re-create the ambience of this wonderful era with contemporary needs in mind.

Photo © Rich Frutchey

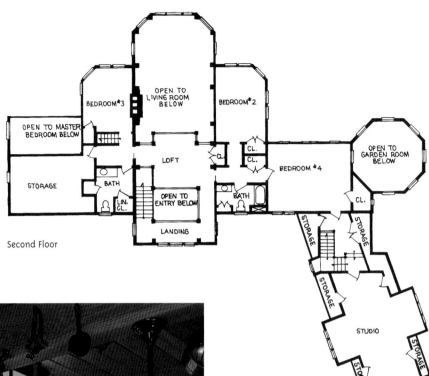

Second Floor

thaw turns the road to the building site into impassable muck. Even when everything is going right, opening day for deer or trout season can throw a wrench into your carefully planned schedule. The key to keeping a project moving along with a minimum of frustration is to work with contractors and tradesmen who have reputations for solving problems and for managing their projects calmly and efficiently.

Finally, understand that any time you go off on your own, you're adding a measure of difficulty that you might not experience in an ordinary project, but your reward will be greater for the satisfaction you'll feel when it's done. You'll also have a home to cherish as much for what you put into it as for what you'll get out of it.

Photo © Rich Frutchey

Heating large-volume, high-ceilinged rooms like this can be difficult with conventional hydronic (hot-water) or forced-air systems, and ceiling fans do little to return rising hot air to floor levels. An increasingly popular option is to install in-floor radiant heating. Like sunlight on a cold winter day, radiant systems transmit warmth directly to objects and occupants instead of warming the surrounding air.

Although you may not participate in the actual hands-on construction of your home, it pays to understand the people and logistics involved. Septic systems, wells, electrical service, plot lines, easements, and setbacks—all of these items and more require careful attention to detail, as well as the day-to-day tasks of scheduling, installing, inspecting, and, ultimately, problem-solving. How you, your general contractor and your subcontractors cope with these and other matters can make your home in the country a dream come true or a living nightmare.

No one builds a home by oneself, no matter how knowledgeable or skilled one is in the construction trades. It takes a group effort, staffed with any number of laborers and tradesmen, and in today's regulated environment many of those tradesmen must be licensed to perform their highly specialized tasks. If you plan to oversee your own construction project, as many timberframe builders do, you'll need a firsthand understanding of all the members on your team and the tasks they are hired to perform. Here is a short list of the professionals you'll encounter and with whom you will most likely be working.

SURVEYOR

You may not need your own surveyor if your new home is built in a subdivision that has already passed the municipal approval process. However, if you build on a single parcel, you'll want to find a licensed surveyor with a solid local reputation, because his work will be critical to your building program from the first day onward. Having your property surveyed is most important if it is virgin land or if it's part of a larger parcel that dates back to antiquity. To help you avoid costly disputes, which are common in such situations, a survey is required to reconfirm lot lines or find boundary markers, if any exist. Surveyors also plot elevations, stake out the building site, grade roads and driveways, and mark the locations of septic systems and wells.

It is often the little things that catch the eye and make the big elements work. Note how the vertical posts connect with the horizontal beams at a slight angle. The girts, or braces, are milled with a sweeping arch at the lower side that gives them a look reflective of an oak tree. Notice how moldings where the posts meet the floor soften the edges and create a transition point.

Photo © Franklin Schmidt

Second Level

OPEN BELOW

BEDROOM

MASTER BEDROOM

BATH

BALCONY

BEDROOM

WIC

SHOWER

BATH

LINEN

ROBBIE RESIDENCE
SECOND LEVEL

TV ROOM

GREAT ROOM

DINING ROOM

BATH

BEDROOM

ENTRY

PR

KITCHEN

Main Level

CABINETS

GARAGE

DEN

ENTERTAINMENT
CENTER
WET BAR

BATH

BEDROOM

UTILITY

Basement

Producer: Hearthstone, Inc.

Designer: Mark Kirkpatrick

Built at an elevation of more than 4,000 feet, this timberframe home was engineered to withstand winds in excess of 150 miles per hour—yet there is not one metal fastener in the mortise-and-tenon, solid-oak frame. In addition to strength and stability, owner Dan Robbie wanted his mountaintop retreat to meld with the site and reflect the nature of its impressive surroundings—North Carolina's Beech Mountain, Grandfather Mountain, and Sugar Mountain. To meet the challenge, designer-builder Mark Kirkpatrick responded with a design that includes a towering central mass whose peaks are repeated in the entryway dormers and nearby summits. The fieldstone façade completes the architectural statement that clearly says this is a mountain home. Of note is the way the exterior motif is repeated on the interior with a twenty-eight-foot-high cathedral ceiling, floor-to-ceiling fieldstone fireplace, and a gracefully curved main staircase with open steps that are rough-hewn from hefty half logs.

The south-facing windows are part of a passive solar scheme in which the white floor tiles absorb the heat during the day and radiate it back at night. Coupled with insulated shades that can be lowered at night, the house is able to retain its warmth. The wood-stove is set into a soapstone extension of the kitchen counter that is gently heated by the stove and keeps serving dishes warm during meal times.

STOCKWELL HOUSE

Producer: Yankee Barn Homes

Designer: Arne Rebne

The cedar-shake roof and stone façade give this gambrel-roofed home the secure look of a country barn. Note how well the gambrel roofline increases the volume and spaciousness of the interior. This northern exposure, with its protected windows, is a sharp contrast to the expansive light color of the contemporary interior, where room divisions are only hinted at through the configuration of overhead beams. The twin cupolas serve as venting for the woodstove.

CIVIL ENGINEER

If your property is too remote to tie into a municipal sewer district, you'll need a waste-treatment facility of some type—usually an in-ground septic tank or leaching field—and a locally approved engineer to design it. The plan may be drawn up by the surveying company or by an engineering firm that specializes in this work. The engineer who designs the system is usually responsible for securing health department approval of both the plans and its final construction.

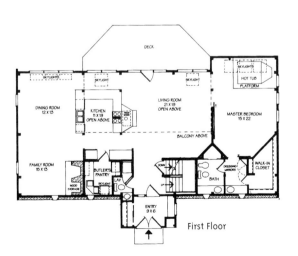

First Floor

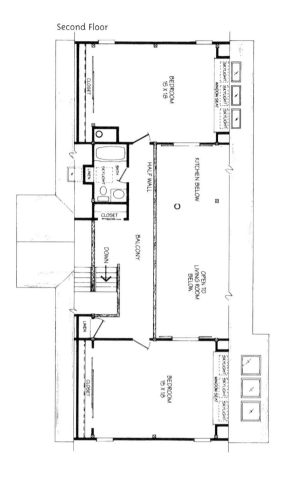

Second Floor

Photo © Vincent Lisanti

MUNICIPAL INSPECTORS

Local building, fire, and health officials regulate home construction in most areas of the country today. They are empowered to enforce standards typically based on national model codes such as the Uniform Building Code and the National Electrical Code. These departments issue permits and require inspections at various stages during construction.

ARCHITECT

Many homes are designed and built without architects, and sometimes architects are hired to design and oversee the entire project. Depending on your needs and budget, you can hire an architect to work

A whirlpool in the master bedroom allows the owners a chance to indulge in sensual pleasures while gazing at the stars through the many windows and skylights in this private retreat.

Photo © Suki Coughlin

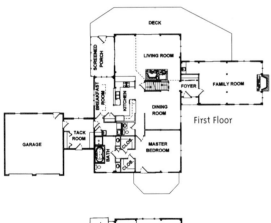

First Floor

Second Floor

SEIDEL HOUSE

Producer: Yankee Barn Homes

Designer: Jim Wheeler

This house is designed for one-floor living. The guest quarters are upstairs, as is the sewing room and office. For summertime outdoor living, the owners created both a screened-in porch and a beautiful deck that surrounds the signature Palladian windows.

on any or every phase of your home's construction, from the initial concept through to its completion. Some municipalities require a state-licensed architect's or engineer's seal on your building plans, or accept homes designed to meet national building codes. Before you apply for a building permit, check your area's requirements. Even minor modifications to approved plans may require a local architect's or engineer's certification.

INTERIOR DESIGNER

After the architect designs your home, this subcontractor may be called in to plan and

supervise construction in specific areas, such as the kitchen and baths, or to create an overall décor and furnishing scheme throughout the home's interior. Many designers are trained and certified by professional organizations such as the American Society of Interior Designers or the National Kitchen & Bath Association. If you intend to hire a designer, have your plans reviewed early in the process; it could save lots of headaches later and result in a more satisfying home.

GENERAL CONTRACTOR

Among the designers, subcontractors, tradesmen, and suppliers that march through every home-building project, there is only one general contractor, or GC. This key player (also referred to simply as the builder) orders the materials, hires the various tradesmen or subcontractors and coordinates their work, arranges for permits and inspections, and is responsible for virtually every decision in all phases of construction.

The posts and beams create a wall-less division within a single room, which allows for a variety of activities—ranging from playing pool to relaxing by the fire—to take place simultaneously.

The contemporary use of space offers privacy in the bedrooms, but keeps the overall home integrated through the use of half walls on the second story. This is definitely a home that works well for either vacation or year-round living.

Photo © Michael Penney

Producer: Habitat Post & Beam

Designer: Ann H. Renehan

This small Cape Cod-inspired home is available in models as small as 1,750 square feet to the largest at just under 2,400 square feet. Though the exterior—with its vernacular design, modest windows, and narrow clapboards—bespeaks the modest homes of the Cape and Islands off the Massachusetts coast, the interior gives way to modern lifestyle requirements. Ann H. Renehan's design offers a feeling that is far bigger than the square footage indicates. In all, the design is straightforward, honest, and functional, resulting in quiet understated elegance.

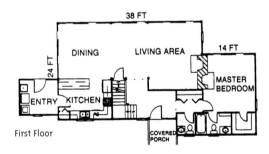

First Floor

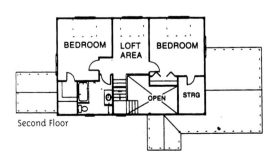

Second Floor

CONSTRUCTION MANAGER

When owners decide to build their own home and act as general contractor, they are wise to hire an experienced contractor to assist them. A part-time construction manager can help plan each phase of the project, supervise subcontractors, manage operations that are unfamiliar to the owners, and be on the job when the owner is unavailable. Freelance managers are often retired general contractors who will work part-time on an hourly or flat-fee basis.

CORNISH HOLLOW/ARCHER JACKSON

Producer: Lindal Cedar Homes

This home's horizontal layout is appropriate for its wide-open setting. The low roofline doesn't obstruct the sweeping views. Though two stories high, it is built in a ranch style that won't lose as much interior warmth to cold winter winds. The large roof overhangs shade the walls and windows from strong sunlight in summer while allowing the welcome light from a low winter sun to shine in. Wide roof rakes and eaves deflect rain and snow as well, which helps to protect siding and foundation plantings.

Photo © Lindal Cedar Homes

Second Floor

First Floor

SUBCONTRACTORS

EXCAVATOR—provides the heavy equipment used to clear the site, dig and backfill the foundation, and regrade the landscape after construction is complete. Because this equipment is costly to operate and is needed at several stages of the job, an excavator is often one of the most important and expensive subs on the job.

CONCRETE MASON—handles all manner of concrete placement, including the construction of footings, foundations, walls, and flat work such as patios, walks, and driveways. Some masons specialize in brick or block construction, exterior

Nice touches in this kitchen include a window that functions as a mini-greenhouse for growing herbs and a wood ceiling.

stucco, fireplace construction, and interior decorative work such as tile setting.

CARPENTER—is responsible for the basic wood
framing and construction, including the installation of windows and interior and exterior
doors. Carpentry may be divided between separate subcontractors for rough framing, roofing, siding, flooring, interior trim, cabinetry
and built-ins, etc.

ELECTRICIAN—installs all interior electrical
components such as basic wiring, switches,
outlets, and fixtures, including bringing power
to the house from the utility pole or meter. He
also arranges for the required electrical inspections and permits, which are separate from
building, plumbing, and health inspections.
The electrician may also install the wiring and
receptacles for the telephone and coaxial
cable-television wiring.

Timberframe construction lends itself to remarkable interiors, including rooms of unusual proportions such as this octagon. Nonstandard-sized or -shaped rooms can be a challenge to build and can wreak havoc with interior planning. When designing your dream home, be smart and give some thought to where you'll place important items like furniture and electrical outlets.

CURRY HOME

Producer: Hearthstone, Inc.

Architect: Chris Wood

The extended prow roof on this house provides shade in the summer and protects the large glass areas from wind-driven rain, which can increase maintenance chores over time. All wood in this home was cut from eastern white pine that has been hand-hewn and weather-aged, a Hearthstone process that raises the grain to give the structure a two-hundred-year-old appearance. In many cases, Hearthstone purchases timber rights in land that is at high elevations where the longest and straightest trees grow.

Photo © Harley Ferguson

PLUMBER—installs all freshwater plumbing and drains, waste and vent (DWV) sewer lines, as well as the faucets and porcelain fixtures (sinks, tubs, and toilets). This subcontractor may also install the plumbing for the home's heating system and is responsible for all tests and inspections required by the plumbing or health code.

HVAC—designs and installs the interior ductwork, air handlers, and other equipment for forced-air heating, ventilating, and air-conditioning systems.

The home was designed as a hybrid, with sleeping and other areas done in solid log and the great room done in timberframe construction. Chinking, normally used to fill in gaps between logs in exterior walls, is used on this solid-log interior wall to produce a more rustic environment. This wall serves to divide the timberframe and log portions of the home.

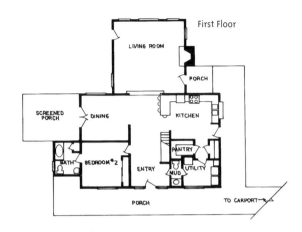

First Floor

Second Floor

DRYWALLER—installs and finishes interior wall surfaces such as gypsum board or plaster. This job may be done by a drywall specialist, by the carpenters after framing is complete, or by a painting and plastering subcontractor.

PAINTER—takes care of interior and exterior painting, staining, and application of wood sealers or preservatives. The painter's job may include plastering the interior, spackling the drywall, and touching up, as well as caulking exposed joints on exterior walls, doors, and windows.

Hand-hewn and weathered trusses span this great room and are configured in a manner that lends a more horizontal feeling to the space. The feeling is reinforced in the windows that look over a vista of North Carolina's Great Smoky Mountains. Modern "low-e glass" makes it possible to have immense windows without paying a penalty in energy costs.

CASE HOUSE

Producer: Lindal Cedar Homes

Located in horse country, this home is designed to take in views of expansive grazing land from a second-story deck that extends the entire length of the magnificent residence. There are also a first-floor porch and a ground-level patio to take in the pastoral setting. Most importantly, the Cases resisted the impulse to build at the crest of a rolling hill, and instead nestled the home lower into the terrain. In terms of their view, nothing was lost, while the natural beauty of the Virginia countryside was preserved.

This view demonstrates just how large of an interior expanse can be created in a well-engineered timberframe home.

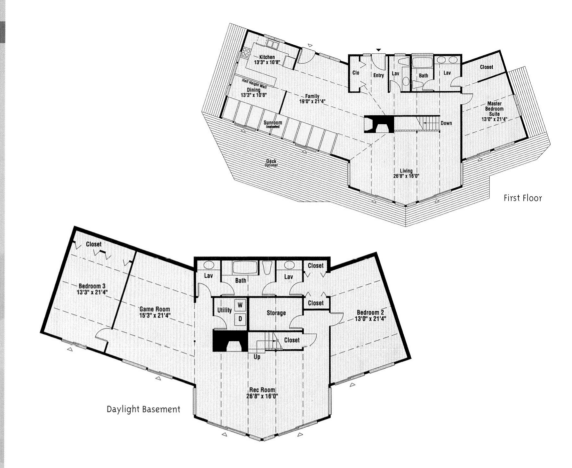

First Floor

Daylight Basement

Photo © Lindal Cedar Homes

WASTE HAULER—construction-site cleanup and trash disposal is critical during construction, and today it is often regulated by the local municipality. Rented waste dumpsters are dropped at the site by the hauler and picked up when full. These containers are sized and priced by the cubic yard, with disposal or dump fees included in the price.

Photo © Don Kerkhof

Trees in nineteenth-century America were pretty much taken for granted. But today, an old-growth red oak on a timberframe building site may be the only one of its kind. If the tree is damaged, replacing it is impossible, and coming even close with a mature hardwood tree will cost a minimum of $5,000 to purchase and plant and will take a decade to develop any character.

Fortunately, there are experts whose disciplines can play a vital role in preserving the visual appeal and health of a nicely forested lot. They are architects—including landscape architects who will integrate the new home with its unique surroundings, and licensed or certified arborists who will protect valuable trees during construction and maintain their health and beauty for years to come.

Certified arborist Steve Bevilacqua, president of Timber Tree Corporation, in Canton, Massachusetts, explains, "The first order of business is to know what trees you have. Walk the proposed site with an arborist who will identify the trees and advise on which ones are valuable in terms of aesthetics and replacement costs, and which ones—such as poplar—should be removed because they are unattractive or will topple easily, posing a danger."

Bevilacqua recommends contacting the National Arborist Association, Inc., in Amherst, New Hampshire, for qualified individuals who can make decisions about the care and protection of trees on the building site. These individuals will inventory the trees—especially within view of the house—and will plan the removal of those that must go and preserve those worth keeping.

Another asset the homeowner might discover is an occasional old fruit tree or an abandoned orchard. "When these trees are neglected, they will bear fruit sporadically. However, with severe pruning and annual fertilizing, the productive life of these trees can be renewed." And an added benefit—apple wood is great for burning.

GALEWYRICK HOUSE

Producer: Hearthstone, Inc.

This home's owner is a sculptor and painter as well as a medical doctor. He began working on the design while in college and, after fifteen years, began construction. He participated as general contractor and worked weekends and evenings to make his dream come true—a magnificent hilltop home overlooking Rice Lake in Wisconsin. The traditional stucco cladding is a durable material made of cement with an aggregate whose size determines textures and color, which can be modified by adding mineral oxide pigments to the mix. Taken as a whole, this home underscores how several traditional building materials—wood, brick, stucco, and slate—can join together in perfect color and textural harmony.

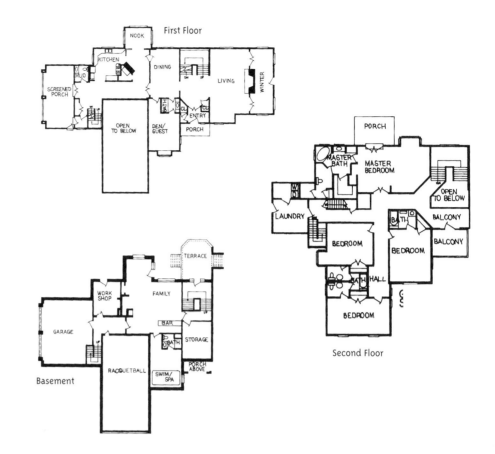

Photo © Don Kerkhof

Consulting with an arborist, including walking the site, identifying trees, and reviewing various strategies to establish and maintain a desired look, will cost from $200 to $400.

THE LANDSCAPE ARCHITECT'S PERSPECTIVE

Integrating the living space—including outdoor living space—with the existing environment is the focus of both landscape and building architects, with the former focusing predominantly on the outdoors. The American Society of Landscape Architects suggests involving a

100

The post-and-beam structure surrounding the grand open staircase gives this home a lofty airy feeling. Note how the extended landing gives one a crow's-nest view of the interior. To soften the look, there are a number of gently curved braces to offset the horizontal and vertical white-oak timbers.

NYGAARD HOME

Designer/Producer: Classic Post & Beam

This home in Greenwich, Connecticut, is a study in contrasts. Owner Odvar Nygaard chose the elegance of a post-and-beam interior and combined it with the ruggedness of a log exterior that hearkens back to his Scandinavian roots. To achieve the look he wanted, Nygaard purchased a kit from Classic Post & Beam, whose parent company, Northeastern Log Homes, provided the natural log siding. Through the creative use of post-and-beam engineering, a living room with a thirty-foot span was created along with a second-floor lounge, whose openness and views give it a porch-like feeling. As the home frequently accommodates friends and relatives from abroad, having such a space right off the guest bedrooms is ideal. Guests can get away from the great room to read or visit in small groups but are still close enough to the dining room. The double-door entryway leading to a massive fieldstone fireplace and great room is another visual element that underscores the welcoming nature of the home and its owner.

Photo © George Riley

landscape architect early in the project to analyze the land's natural features, including topography and geological features such as rock outcroppings, streams and ponds, wetlands, and so forth. The goal is to develop a comprehensive site plan that preserves natural features and locates development where it will create the least impact on the environment. Early involvement by an ASLA professional will prevent mistakes and open up new options for the owner.

For a variety of reasons—not the least of which is cost—you may not want to implement all of the landscape ideas immediately. Develop a plan based on the site and your lifestyle, then it can be implemented over time or revised due to changing needs. The ASLA can provide lists of local professionals. Hire someone who cares about what you care about and who shares your vision.

First Floor

Second Floor

SITING THE HOUSE

When discussing the actual site for the house, the architect will introduce ideas about how the house and land will work in harmony so that the house won't become a foreign object in a natural surrounding. There are practical considerations too, such as building on a steep slope to take advantage of a vista. If the home is for retirement, consider the disadvantage of negotiating a lot of stairs and steep grades.

In a northern climate, the home should be designed to take advantage of a southern exposure. In winter, when the sun is low and

A hefty chopping block is a focal point in this kitchen, where seafood is the order of the day—from a unique marinated baked salmon to a native lobster dinner complete with steamers, chowder, and corn on the cob.

The décor is country traditional; the white walls and a white-painted brick fireplace lend a contemporary feeling to the living space. Note how a raised hearth adds dimension to the interior structure. The placement of a natural-wood batten door with wrought-iron hinges right next to a kitchen with white-enamel cabinets demonstrates how stained wood next to bold colors, or warm wood next to cool tiles, can give the timberframe home its pizzazz.

Top Level

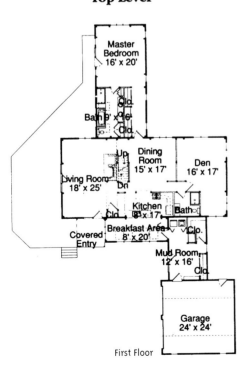

First Floor

Producer: Yankee Barn

Designer: Bruce Parsons

One way to fully appreciate the benefits of a timberframe home is to stay in one. That's exactly what Dorothy and Paul McCusker did before settling on their home. After spending a weekend at Yankee Barn's Gathering House, the McCuskers decided to eliminate a second-story loft and take full advantage of the openness and symmetry offered by an uninterrupted cathedral ceiling. To help customers visualize the design process, the manufacturer provides quarter-scale solid-wood building blocks. The blocks give one a sense for the volume of the home and for numerous configurations, using extensions of various sizes. Moving the pieces around brings the design into sharper focus. It is a very hands-on way to design one's dream home.

deciduous trees have lost their leaves, the sun can provide warmth. In summer, when the sun is higher, leafy trees and large projecting eaves will help keep the home cool. Nick Winton, a principal in the architecture firm of Anmahian Winton Associates in Cambridge, Massachusetts, advises, "If possible, don't make judgments about siting the home based on a summer visit. Winter reveals features that may not be apparent when the trees are leafed out."

Architects' fees range from 10 to 15 percent of the cost of construction, or a fixed or hourly fee can be negotiated. Since most timberframe

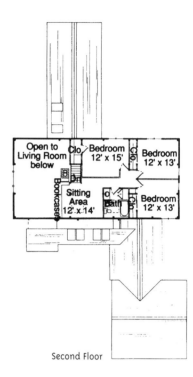

Open to Living Room below | Clo. | Bedroom 12' x 15' | Cl | Bedroom 12' x 13'

Bookcase

Sitting Area 12' x 14' | Bath | Bedroom 12' x 13'

Second Floor

manufacturers will prepare blueprints and a "punch list," it is helpful to have the architect and manufacturer coordinate their areas of responsibility early in the project.

When it comes to a wooded site, working with an architect, landscape architect, and arborist will surely result in a project in which the beauty of the site and the home do not compete for the starring role, but share time in the limelight.

JACKSON HOLE

Designer: Goddard Construction

Architect: Danny Eagan

Located in the Grand Teton Mountains, this stunning home combines truss work on a grand scale with an eye-popping roofline silhouetted against the mountain peaks. Though there are more than 6,000 square feet of living space, architect Danny Eagan created a cleverly angled floor plan that is intimate and cozy.

Photo © Roger Wade

TREES ADD VALUE

According to the National Arborist Association, Inc., headquartered in Amherst, New Hampshire, a well-maintained landscape with mature trees can increase property values up to 25 percent. The organization offers the following advice:

•Trees cool houses in the summer.

•Trees warm houses in the winter by blocking wind.

The truss design in
this area is repeated
to create an overall
theme that
emphasizes height
and draws the eye
to the splendid
outdoor vistas.

First Floor

Second Floor

•Trees reduce air pollution.

•Trees reduce noise pollution.

•Trees reduce erosion.

•Trees improve visual appeal.

•Trees attract wildlife.

•Trees provide privacy.

When building a two-story home with potential for views, consider an upside-down floor plan, with the main living area on the upper stories and the bedrooms on the first floor. This takes full advantage of views, increases natural light, and gives the living areas the more dramatic ceilings and trusswork.

Despite this home's mass, its owners created a nestled-in look by situating it within a backdrop of stately trees and using plenty of glass to bring the outside in.

Photo © Brad Simmons

Producer: Yankee Barn Homes

Designer: Arne Rebne

The owners wanted a second home that wasn't a cookie-cutter design, brought in lots of light, and made them feel connected to the outdoors. And since the couple loves old barns, Yankee Barn Homes was the perfect choice. This company has been designing and manufacturing custom post-and-beam homes since 1969, using reclaimed antique timbers to create homes with soaring cathedral ceilings and cozy lofts that are rooted in the American barn. The high ceilings create volume, which increases the sense of space markedly, while the old beams give the home its charm, character, warmth, and intimacy.

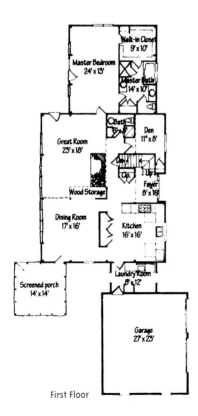

First Floor

FREE LITERATURE

The International Society of Arboriculture, a non-profit organization supporting tree-care research around the world and dedicated to the care and preservation of shade and ornamental trees, offers free plant-care brochures that cover a wide range of topics. Literature has been developed as a joint project between the Utility Arborist Association and the International Society of Arboriculture. The ASLA, which provides listings of Professional Landscape Architects throughout the United States, offers the following advice:

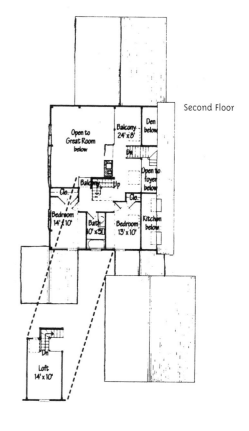

Second Floor

•Analyze the site and develop a site plan before changing the grade or removing any existing plants and trees.

• If your goal is to live in the country, avoid re-creating a suburban environment.

•Find out how big the tree will grow before planting. Too many homeowners have made the mistake of using trees for foundation plantings that will grow to thirty-feet in diameter.

•Consider alternatives to formal lawns.

•Other points to consider: outdoor entertainment areas; unobtrusive spaces for parking cars; outdoor lighting; preservation and enhancement of existing features such as ponds and streams.

•Be creative: respond to the site and create your dream.

Left: In most families, members want to be able to escape to private areas but still want to keep up with what's going on in the public spaces. Second- and third-level balconies that integrate private areas with the great room achieve this. The owners used a contrasting color for the beams to emphasize the structure.

Although this home office is tucked into a small space under a sloping ceiling, the inclusion of a skylight gives it an open feeling, adding lots of light and ventilation.

Bay—The open area created between bents, or any open space within a framework.

Beam—Any horizontal wood member larger than three inches in width and four inches in depth; this term also refers specifically to a structural component that supports other horizontal members, such as floor joists; variations include girding beams, summer beams, and tie beams.

Bent—An essential unit in timberframe and post-and-beam construction. It is composed of at least two posts and a beam, but is often made up of any number of structural members. Like the individual slices in a loaf of bread, bents often extend completely through a structure from outside wall to outside wall and from sill plate to ridge.

Brace—A frame-support member, set at an angle between a post and a beam, that is used to prevent frame racking or twisting; also called an angle brace, knee brace, or wind brace.

Chamfer—An angled cut (usually forty-five degrees) along the squared edge of a post or beam that is often used for decoration and to relieve the sharp corner where it may come into contact with people or objects. A chamfer with a complex design or profile is referred to as a bead; a chamfer that extends to a specific point and then tapers off is called a stopped chamfer.

Chord—The principal horizontal beam(s) in a truss assembly.

Collar tie—A connecting beam between two rafters, perpendicular to the ridge; ties help prevent rafter sag and outward pressure, or thrust, on top-wall plates; also referred to as tie beams or tie collars.

Crown—The natural convex bow in a beam of any length; when the beam is positioned, its crowned face is turned upward to prevent sagging.

Deck—Any weight-bearing horizontal surface in a structure, including the floors, roof, and exterior extensions.

Drying—The process of removing excess water and sap from cut wood. Air drying allows wood to lose moisture naturally over a period of months or years, depending on the wood thickness and species; kiln drying uses dehumidification and increased air temperature to achieve the same effect in a much shorter time.

Gable—A triangular rafter assembly that converges in a peak.

Girts—The main horizontal beams, also called girding beams or girders, that span the width or length of a frame; variations include bent girts, connecting girts, and sill girts.

Gunstock—A post that is flared (wider) at one end to provide extra strength or support, such as where a post top is required to carry a large and complex intersection of other timbers; also referred to as a haunch or joweled post.

Joists—Horizontal beams that support the floors, usually connected at each end to a girt or intermediary summer beam, or supported from below by a floor beam or girder.

Mill Construction—A standard fire-code designation applied to larger timbers with a minimum cross-section of eight inches on each face or side.

Plate—An assembly of beams that forms a perimeter at the bottom (base or sill plate) and upper tier (top plate) of a frame, encompassing the entire structure; a raising plate is an additional horizontal member positioned atop the attic-floor joists that creates a base for the rafter ends.

Posts—The vertical "legs," or supports, of a post-and-beam framework. Corner posts are key elements, usually extending from the sill plate to the top plate. Intermediary posts may be positioned anywhere within the frame to add support. Queen posts are twin symmetrical frame members spaced apart within a roof truss, extending down from the rafters to the lower truss chord, or collar tie. A king post is the central vertical element in a truss.

Purlin—A connecting beam placed perpendicular to the roof rafters; purlins supported by the principal rafters create a horizontal framework that eliminates the need for secondary rafters; a purlin installed at the midpoint below the rafters provides support and allows for shorter rafter lengths.

Rafters—Roof-support members that extend from the top wall plate to the ridge, generally at a sloping angle that determines the roof pitch; depending on their position, rafters are referred to as common rafters, major rafters, principal rafters, or secondary rafters.

Ridge—The top horizontal beam that forms the house peak with the rafters; also called a ridge beam, ridge plate, or ridgepole.

Span—The unsupported distance between two load-bearing members. Construction-code span tables, based on engineering calculations that anticipate loads and the wood species used, list the allowable limits between structural supports.

Timber—Any length of wood with a cross-section greater than five inches on each face or side.

Truss—A geometric assembly of posts and beams that transfers the weight of a roof or upper-story section—such as a balcony or loft—to the walls without support from below; variations include hammer-beam truss, king- and queen-post trusses, and scissor truss.

These plans and photos of post-and-beam and timberframe homes are your foundation. They are presented to inspire, encourage, and stimulate your creativity as you take the first steps toward turning your dream home into a reality. We urge you to talk with as many experts as you can, as well as those who have built and live in these homes. Consider it a journey along which you will develop a sense for a home that is both in tune with your aesthetic values and which meets the practical needs of your lifestyle.

And, though the roots of timberframing are intricate and deep, your home will add to the state of the art and, perhaps, become the tradition of tomorrow.

Here are selected sources that offer additional information to help guide you in your own building project.

PROFESSIONAL ASSOCIATIONS

Building Systems Council of NAHB
1201 - 15th Street NW
Washington, DC 20005
800-368-5242
info@NAHB.com

National Association of Home Builders
1201 - 15th Street NW
Washington, DC 20005
800-368-5242
info@NAHB.com

Structural Insulated Panel Association
253-858-7472
253-858-0272 fax
staff@sips.org

Timber Framers Guild
Joel McCarty and Will Beemer,
Executive Directors
P.O. Box 60
Becket, MA 01223
888-453-0879 phone/fax
info@tfguild.org

The American Society of Landscape Architects
4401 Connecticut Avenue NW
Washington, DC 20008
202-686-2752
www.asla.org/asla/

International Society of Arboriculture
P.O. Box GG
Savoy, IL 61874-9902

National Arborist Association, Inc.
P.O. Box 1094
Manchester, NH 03031
800-733-2622

MAGAZINES

Timber Frame Homes Magazine
Home Buyer Publications
4200-T Lafayette Center Drive
Chantilly, VA 20151
800-826-3893
www.timberframehomes.com

Timber Frame Illustrated Magazine
GCR Publishing
419 Park Avenue South, 18th Floor
New York, NY 10016
800-442-1869
212-245-1241 fax

Building Systems Magazine
Home Buyer Publications
4200-T Lafayette Center Drive
Chantilly, VA 20151
800-826-3893

Timber Framing
Timber Framers Guild
P.O. Box 60
Becket, MA 01223
888-453-0879 phone/fax
info@tfguild.org

Joiners Quarterly
Fox Maple Press
P.O. Box 249
Brownfield, ME 04010
207-935-3720

Fine Homebuilding
Taunton Press
P.O. Box 355
Newtown, CT 06470

NEWSLETTERS

Scantlings
Newsletter of the Timber Framers Guild
P.O. Box 60
Becket, MA 01223
888-453-0879

Summer Beam Books
(catalog with 250-300 titles on timberframing)
2299 Route 488
Clifton Springs, NY 14432
877-272-1987

VIDEOS

Timber Framers Guild
P.O. Box 60
Becket, MA 01223
888-453-0879

The Timber Framers Guild offers the following videotapes.

Timber Frame: The Complete Video.
A 55-minute video that features a general overview of timberframe construction and includes historical background, building terminology, explanations of joinery and raising the frame, interior views, and information on historic restoration and replication. Cost: $30 U.S. plus $3 shipping.

**Covered Bridge:
400 Timber Framers Build a Bridge.**
A 55-minute video about the guild's volunteer effort to build a 120-foot pedestrian lattice-covered bridge over the Speed River in Guelph, Ontario. Some 400 people raised by hand the two large side trusses of the bridge, assembled the roof, and later pushed the completed bridge into position over the river.
Cost: $30 U.S. plus $3 shipping.

Timber Frame Barn Raising, 1929.
A 24-minute video with archival footage of a traditional barn raising, the celebration that followed, and recollections of three people who took part in the raising in July 1929. Cost: $25 U.S. plus $3 shipping.

Timber Frame Gazebo.
A 20-minute video that records the cutting of a gazebo frame by members of the Timber Framers Guild in Canada. They used the traditional French scribe method, with plumb lines and levels, to build the 20' x 30' gazebo.
Cost: $20 U.S. plus $3 shipping.

TIMBERFRAMING TOOLS

POWER TOOLS

Mafell Carpentry and Woodworking Tools
Mafell North America
Dennis Hambruch
80 Earhart Drive, Unit 9
Williamsville, NY 14221
716-626-9303
716 626-9304 fax

Makita Tools
Russ Williams
Barn Masters
P.O. Box 258
Freeport, ME 04032
207-865-4169
207-865-6169 fax
info@barnmasters.com

HAND TOOLS

Barr Specialty Tools
P.O. Box 4335
McCall, ID 83638
208- 634-3641
www.barrtools.com

Garrett Wade Co.
161 Avenue of the Americas
New York, NY 10013
800-221-2942

Hida Tool and Hardware Co.
1333 San Pablo Avenue
Berkeley, CA 94702
415-524-3500 fax

Lee Valley Tools, Ltd.
2680 Queensview Drive
Ottawa, ON K2B 8H6
Canada
613-596-0350

Whole Earth Access
822 Anthony Street
Berkeley, CA 94710

Woodcraft Supply
210 Wood County Industrial Park
P.O. Box 1686
Parkersburg, WV 26102
800-225-1153

Woodline, the Japan Woodworker
1731 Clement Avenue
Alameda, CA 94501

TIMBERFRAME AND POST-AND-BEAM COMPANIES

Classic Post & Beam
P.O. Box 546
York, ME 03909
Contact: James Nadeau
800-872-2326
207-363-2411 fax
www.classicpostandbeam.com
info@classicpostandbeam.com

Deck House, Inc.
930 Main Street
Acton, MA 01720
800-727-3325
www.deckhouse.com

Jack A. Sobon, Timberframer
P.O. Box 201
Windsor, MA 01270
413-684-3223

George Senerchia
Barn Restorations and Timberframes
109 Old Post Road
Northford, CT 06472
203-484-2129

Normerica Building Systems Inc.
Sam Kewen, Sales Manager
150 Ram Forest Road
Gormely, ON L0H 1G0
Canada
800-361-7449
905-841-9061 fax
www.normerica.com
info@normerica.com

Davis Frame Co.
P.O. Box 1079
Rte 12A South
Claremont, NH 03743
800-636-0993
603-543-0993 fax

Oakbridge Timber Framing
John Miller or Jim Kanagy
20857 Earnest Road
Howard, OH 43028
740-599-5711

Riverbend Timber Framing
Frank Baker
P.O. Box 26
Blissfield, MI 49228
517-486-4355
517-486-2056 fax
www.riverbendtf.com
Frank@rtfgli.clrs.com
-Timber frames and panel-engineered packages, timberframe erection, panel installation.
Market Area: National/International

The Cascade Joinery
Ross Grier
1401 Sixth Street
Bellingham, WA 98225
360-527-0119
360-527-0142 fax
www.cascadejoinery.com
info@cascadejoinery.com
-Complete design services, frame fabrication and installation, SIP enclosure.
Market Area: Worldwide

Timbercraft Homes, Inc.
Charles Landau
85 Martin Road
Port Townsend, WA 98368
360-385-3051
360-385-7745 fax
www.timbercraft.com
info@timbercraft.com

Timberpeg
Bob Best
P.O. Box 5474
W. Lebanon, NH 03784
603-298-8820
603-298-5425 fax
www.timberpeg.com
info@timberpeg.com

Vermont Timberframes
Tom Harrison
7 Pearl Street
Cambridge, NY 12816
518-677-8860
518-677-3626 fax
www.vtf.com
tomharrison@vtf.com

Dreaming Creek Timber Frame Homes
Robert Shortridge
2487 Judes Ferry Road
Powhatan, VA 23139
804-598-4328
804-598-3748 fax
www.dreamingcreek.com
DCTFH@aol.com

HearthStone
Carmen Capio
1630 E. Hwy 25-70
Dandridge, TN 37725
865-397-9425
865-397-9262 fax
www.hearthstonehomes.com
ccaprio@hearthstonehomes.com

Vermont Timber Works
Doug Friant, Dan Kelleher, and Kimberly Morse
P.O. Box 856
Springfield, VT 05156
802-885-1917
802-885-6188 fax
www.VermontTimberWorks.com

Yankee Barn Homes
Rob Knight
131 Yankee Barn Road
Grantham, NH 03753
800-258-9786
603-863-4551 fax
www.yankeebarnhomes.com
info@yankeebarnhomes.com

The Murus Company
Linda Lee
P.O. Box 220
Route 549
Mansfield, PA 16933
570-549-2101 fax
www.murus.com
murus@epix.net
-Structural insulated panels.

Mountain Construction Enterprises, Inc.
Mark Kirkpatrick
P.O. Box 1177
Boone, NC 28607
828-264-1231
828-264-4863 fax
www.mountainconstruction.com
mtnconst@boone.net

New Energy Works Timberframers
Housewrights & Joiners
1180 Commercial Drive
Farmington, NY 14425
800-486-0661
716-924-9962 fax
www.newenergyworks.com

Habitat Post & Beam
21 Elm Street
S. Deerfield, MA 01373
800 992-0121
413-665-4008 fax
www.postandbeam.com

Bear Creek Timberwrights
1934 Middle Bear Creek Road
P.O. Box 335
Victor, MT 59875
406-642-6003
406-642-6005 fax
www.bearcreektimber.com

Lindal Cedar Homes, Inc.
4300 S. 104th Place
Seattle, WA 98178
OR
P.O. Box 24426
Seattle, WA 98124
800-426-0536
www.Lindal.com

Pacific Post & Beam
P.O. Box 13708
San Luis Obispo, CA 93406
805-543-7565
www.pacificpostbeam.com

ARCHITECTS

Duo Dickinson
Madison, CT 06443
203-245-0405

Danny Eagan
Jackson Hole, WY 83001
307-733-8821

Nick Winton
Cambridge, MA 02140
617-997-6600